My Childhood Series
# Growing Up In East Germany

by Yvonne Jones

ISBN-10: 0997025417
ISBN-13: 978-0-9970254-1-5

Printed in the U.S.A.

Dear Readers,

Telling your little ones about your childhood is a wonderful way to stimulate their imagination while sharing your memorable moments with them. They will discover a piece of your past, hear stories about how the world used to be, and most importantly, learn more about you – their parent, and your history. Sharing your past with your children is one of the most valuable and interesting gifts you could ever bestow upon them. Give it a try and tell them *your* stories.

This collection of tales is the one I recorded for my little ones. They enjoyed it tremendously. They listened to it with so much joy. And they kept on asking for more. Use my stories shared with my children as inspiration to write down your fondest memories of your own childhood, or simply enjoy reading these little stories about days past with your little ones.

*Yvonne Jones*

# CONTENTS

# DEDICATION

To my little sunshine, without whose tireless enthusiasm and support the writing of this book would have never happened.

# 1
# JUST LIVING MY LIFE

So I have heard you are interested in my childhood. Mmmh! So where shall I begin? I have so many exciting stories to tell you! About the creaky apartment I used to live in, about my old school, and about all the fun things I used to do. So we better get to it! Are you ready? Here we go.

My name is Eevi. I was born quite some time ago. The year was 1980. Back then, nobody knew about CDs or DVDs. Very few families even had a computer, and even less knew about the internet. There were not many cellphones – and they were very different to what we have today – and there were definitely no iPads.

Not only was the technology so different, but I even lived in an entirely different country! I was not born in this country you live in today. I was born in the German Democratic Republic, also known as East Germany. But East Germany does not exist as its own country anymore, because it united with West Germany when I was 10 years old.

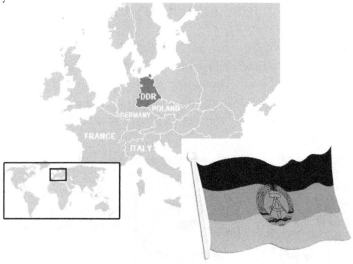

I always liked the flag of our German Democratic Republic. It had three colored stripes, the same as the West German colors: black, red and gold. And our national emblem consisted of a hammer and a compass, encircled with rye. The hammer represented the workers in our factories. The compass stood for the academics, like teachers and students, and the ring of rye represented all our farmers.

When I was a baby, Omama and I lived in this tiny apartment right next to the railroad station. Every time a train passed through, things began to shake and rattle. It was a very noisy place to live in. But I don't really remember because I was too little. I only know these things, because Omama told me about them. We didn't live there for very long, because this apartment was in a very bad condition. Green-looking mold grew on our walls right above my little baby crib – I think it might have even glowed at night! All my life I dreamt about living in a nice house. Having your own house back when I was little was something very special! Most people lived in large apartment buildings, and back then, people couldn't just move wherever and whenever they felt like it. First, they had to ask for permission from the local government. And Omama did. She asked and asked and asked. And after many requests, we were finally allowed to move into another apartment! Omama was very excited, because she was permitted to move into the same apartment building my grandma lived in.

## 2
## OUR LITTLE VILLAGE

I still remember the address of our then-new home, because we lived there until I was about 13 years old. The street name was Glueck-Auf-Siedlung. "Glueck-Auf" used to be a greeting used by coal miners back in the day, meaning 'good luck,' so it felt like a good omen to live on Glueck-Auf Siedlung. Coal miners would say that to each other right before they would go about their dangerous work in old coal mines, deep under the ground. The village our new apartment was in was named Erla. It was very small, with less than 500 people living in it. But I liked it a lot. We had our own post office, our own little grocery store and our own kindergarten. We even had our own little recycling center to which I brought all our collected newspapers and glass all the time. And we had our own little train station, the place Omama worked at every single day. We had a butcher, and right next to it a fancy-looking restaurant. But I never got to eat in there. It was just too fancy for us.

I remember the cute little bakery on our street. When I was about four years old, Omama would put some money and a folded shopping list into my mini-wallet, stuff it into my plaid backpack, set me onto my small blue tricycle and send me down the road to get some rolls for our Saturday breakfast. It wasn't very far; the only road I had to cross was right in front of the house I lived in. So Omama would help me across the street and always tell me to wait for her before crossing back over once I was on my way home. I loved to ride along the bumpy sidewalk. With my two braided pigtails and my favorite backpack, I was on a mission. Of course I couldn't read yet, so when I got to the bakery, I would park my tricycle out front, wait in line, and once it was my turn, I would give the friendly bakery woman Omama's shopping list. She would read it, put the rolls in my backpack, take the money out of the wallet, and send me on my way home.

I felt very important.

During the summer months, I was especially excited

to go to the bakery. You see, our bakery had a window on the side of the building. And when it was extra hot out, they would sell soft, home-made ice cream right out on the street from that window. They had only three flavors: vanilla, chocolate and strawberry. But they never sold all three flavors on the same day. Only one at a time. In my entire childhood, they only opened that window about five times. But when they did, oh boy, would there be a long line of people waiting on the street in front of that window, hoping to get some delicious ice cream.

We bought all our groceries from the small grocery store right across from the bakery. It was called "Konsum." They sold things like fruit, vegetables, laundry detergent, soap, and coffee. But this store didn't look anything like a grocery store you might go to today, full of variety and a hundred different choices to make. We didn't have much to choose from. Going into a store today, you can probably choose from ten different types of jams, or ten different types of bread, or ten different types of soups. We, on the other hand, had only one type of jam, and one type of bread, and one type of soup. When you go into a store today, everything is packed into very colorful boxes and bags. Back then, packaging had no fun colors and no fun characters on them. Milk came in plain glass bottles. Cheese was wrapped in brown paper. Rice and beans were packaged in simple plastic bags. We had no cereal for breakfast, or hamburger helper for dinner. We just had very simple things.

Do you like eating bananas? Well, back when I was little I adored bananas. I thought bananas were the greatest thing in the world. You know why? Because in the German Democratic Republic we only got about one banana a year. It was such a luxury! Can you imagine what it would be like to eat only one banana a year? And whenever our little village sold bananas, a huge line would form in front of the store. We had to patiently wait in line to get our one banana. Banana day was a glorious and exciting day! And once I had my banana, I would eat it very slowly, to be sure to enjoy every single bite.

# 3
# OUR NEW HOME

I didn't tell you very much about my apartment on Glueck-Auf-Siedlung yet. After Omama and I moved, we lived in the same apartment complex as my grandma. The house had three floors, each floor with two apartments. Omama and I lived on the very top floor, right below the attic. And grandma lived on the second floor, right below me and Omama.

Our apartment was very small, so I didn't get to have my own bedroom. I had to sleep with Omama in the same room. We didn't have a bathroom, only a little room with a toilet in it. It wasn't a flushing toilet, but one of those old kinds that looks like an outhouse. In this little room, we had a large pipe coming out of the floor that would lead right into the sewer system. On top of that pipe was a wooden toilet seat. It was very, very, very smelly in that room. In fact, it was so smelly during the heat of summer that you could barely breathe in there. And during the cold winter months, it was so cold that you could see your breath in the air.

Because we didn't have a bathroom, we had a little sink in the kitchen that we would fill up with water in order to wash ourselves. Omama was very resourceful. She put up a curtain in the middle of the kitchen and put an old-fashioned zinc-bathtub behind it. Every Sunday, she would take this enormous pot, fill it with water, and heat it on top of our coal oven. Once it was hot, she would pour the water into our tub. First, I would take a nice long bath with my little bathtub toys, and when I was done, Omama would pour more hot water in the tub and take a bath as well. We couldn't drain the water out of the tub, of course. So after we were done taking our baths, we had to scoop the water out of the tub into the sink. That always took forever.

## 4
## THE DARK BASEMENT

Our house did not have central heating. Instead, each apartment had a coal oven in the kitchen that had to heat the entire apartment. We also used the top of the oven to cook our food every day. In order to use this oven, we had to buy lots and lots of coal. Once a year, they would deliver a truckload of coal to our house. They would dump the entire load into the apartment building's backyard. Imagine a huge pile of dusty, dirty coal in the back of the house! Every apartment had their own storage room in the basement. And every storage room had a tiny little window facing the backyard. So whenever our coal was delivered, everyone would grab big metal shovels and scoop all the coal through the tiny window into the basement. Afterwards, we looked like chimney sweepers, black from head to toe covered in soot and dust.

To keep the apartment warm, we had to burn about a bucketful of coal every day. Remember what floor I lived on? That's right, the very top on the third floor. That meant that every day Omama or I had to go down into the basement with our heavy metal bucket, fill it up with coal, and haul it all the way back up the stairs. During the cold winter months I had to do that every single day. I never liked our basement. It was always cold and dark down there. And very dirty with soot. And there were cobwebs and spiders crawling on the walls and hanging from the ceiling. I never saw any, but I think even some mice lived down there.

But our basement wasn't just for coal storage. We also had a corner in which we stored all our potatoes. That's right: we didn't buy our potatoes in the grocery store. Omama, grandma and I ate so many potatoes every week that we had a huge load delivered about twice a year. Delivery men would bring them in the back of their truck, packed up in very large burlap sacks. We would then drag them into the basement and empty them out into a huge wooden box that stood in the corner of the room. Since our basement was so dark and cold, those potatoes would last practically forever. Once a week I had to go into the basement and haul up a bucket of potatoes for my grandma so she could cook for us.

# 5
# GOOSE FEATHERS

But I'm getting ahead of myself; I wanted to tell you more about our apartment, and what it felt like during the snowy, freezing winter months. Because we only had an oven in the kitchen, our bedroom was always icy cold. It was freezing, actually. And that's why I had this incredibly thick blanket filled with tons and tons of goose feathers. It was so heavy on top of us at night. Every morning, Omama and I had to vigorously shake our bedding to readjust all the feathers in it. Otherwise, they all ended up in one corner of the blanket, leaving none in the other. My pillow was also filled with goose feathers. It was soft, but I always had the pointy end of the feathers poking me.

During the winter, it was so cold that our windows grew icicles on the inside. Can you imagine having icicles on the inside of your window? Sometimes, I could even see my breath in the air. On those days, it was very hard for me to leave my warm and cozy bed. I wore snuggly socks and thick pajamas every night. And sometimes, I even used an extra blanket.

# 6
## OUR COZY EVENINGS

We spent most of our time downstairs in my grandma's apartment. Her apartment was a little bit bigger, with two bedrooms. We would go there for dinner, and also for lunch on the weekends. My grandma cooked all sorts of things; some of them I liked, and some I didn't. I wasn't a very big fan of her weekly stews, for example. But she was a very good cook. Sometimes, on very special occasions, she would also bake a traditional pound cake. When she did, I always liked to lick the spoon.

We spent the evenings together in my grandma's living room; mainly, because she had a huge tile stove in there that kept us warm. A tile stove has tiles attached to all its sides, which helps to keep the room warm and cozy for longer. We would play board games like Sorry or Chinese Checkers, or watch some TV together. My grandma had her very own TV. That was special to us, because Omama and I did not have a TV in our apartment. We only had a radio. We had to watch everything in black and white, because grandma's TV did not have colors. The TV didn't have a remote control, so when we wanted to switch the channel or change the volume, we had to get up and use the buttons and dials on the TV set. But we only had two channels, anyway.

Every night, I would watch this puppet children's program called "Sandmaennchen." I loved it. The little Sandman would come in a different type of vehicle and tell a little bedtime story every night. And right before his departure, he would open his little sack, grab a handful of sand, and spread it all over the room to make all the children sleepy. That's why we sometimes have some 'sand' in our eyes when we wake up in the mornings, or at least that's what they told us when I was little. And after the program was over, I would go back into our own apartment, brush my teeth, change into my pajamas and go to bed. Sometimes, Omama would read a bedtime story to me. Then she would turn off the light, and close the door. When it was time for her to come to bed, she would sneak into the room and find her way back to her side of the bed in the dark.

# 7
# THE AMAZING ATTIC

Omama liked to collect and keep all sorts of things. She never liked to throw things away, because she always thought there might be a day when she would need them. Good thing, then, that we had a humongous attic in the top of the house. Every apartment had their very own room right under the roof of our building. Well, it wasn't really a room, it looked a lot like a large area that was separated by wooden fence-like walls that went from the floor all the way to the ceiling. I loved it, because I could always see what everyone was storing in their little cell. Every cell was lockable with a padlock.

During the summer months, it was always extra hot and stuffy in the attic, because it was right under the roof. We had to climb up these creaky wooden stairs to get up to our belongings. That's where we would store our Christmas decorations and old furniture and things like that. It was always so interesting to look through all the treasures I had forgotten about. One side of the attic floor held the community drying room, which was used to hang up all our wet laundry to let it dry. See, we didn't have dryers back then. We either had to hang our wet laundry on the clotheslines in front of the house, or here in the attic.

# 8
# OUTSIDE FUN

Now that I told you about the inside of our apartment, let me describe what things looked like outside of the house. Every apartment in this house came with its very own garden patch. Right next to the house were six plots, each with its own fence and entrance. Oh, how we loved our garden! We spent so much time in it! And we grew so many things. We had our own strawberries, gooseberries, red currants and black currants. We planted peas and cucumbers and tomatoes. Omama even planted a small plum tree, an apple tree, a pear tree and my favorite, a cherry tree. And we had some flower beds as well. It was beautiful; but also a lot of work. Every weekend, we had to pull weeds or cut the grass, or do some other gardening work. We stored all our gardening tools in a huge wooden wardrobe. It was actually a regular wardrobe that people would use inside an apartment for things like clothes and jackets, but Omama decided to put it outside to have a place to store our tools in. It worked fairly well, but after a while the doors started to creak, and the paint began to peel off. And lots of spiders decided to move in and make it their home. But it worked for our purposes and kept our tools dry.

We also had a teeny tiny garden house. I remember Omama putting a lot of work and pride into it. She built a little bunk bed inside, and decorated the windows and walls with little curtains and picture frames. I always wanted to spend a night in there, because it was just so cute, but Omama never let me. It was too special to her. Right next to it, we had some gardening furniture and a grill. And boy, did we use it a lot! During the warm summer months, we would eat dinner in our garden. It was so wonderful. The air smelled like yummy grilled sausages, music played on the radio, and neighbors and friends chatted the evenings away.

# 9
# MY KIND OF FUN

The most important features in our garden were my very own swing and sandbox. I remember spending so much time in my pink sandbox. My grandpa built it for me when I was very little. He painted it pink just for me and filled it all the way with sand. I had little molds and buckets and sieves to separate the sand from little rocks. I made mud pies and built sandcastles, created mucky rivers and all kinds of fun stuff. My sandbox kept me busy for hours.

And I became quite an acrobat on a swing my grandpa also made me. He used some metal pipes to build the frame and painted it bright red. I would climb up the poles all the way to the very top, pretending to be a fireman when I slid back down. And oh my, did I swing high on that swing! I would sing at the top of my lungs and swing back and forth; swing, swing, swing. Then I would try to see how far I could jump off while it was still in motion. I had a great time.

Right next to the fence in one of the corners of our garden stood a big, old zinc tub. Omama collected rainwater in it so she could water all our plants. One summer it was so hot that Omama decided to turn the tub into a refreshing pool. The cool water felt fantastic in the summer heat. I splashed, floundered and dabbled all about. But then one time, I got a bit boisterous and careless when I decided that it would be a good idea to stand on top of the edges of the tub. Omama tried to warn me, telling me that it was too slippery and that I could get seriously hurt.

But I didn't listen.

And what do you think happened? Omama was

right, of course. One of my feet slipped off the edge, and I landed hard with my chin on the rim of the metal tub. I almost passed out, that's how much it hurt. I still have a small scar on the bottom of my chin to this day.

## 10
## WHO NEEDS A CAR, ANYWAY?

All my childhood, Omama and I survived without a car. Can you imagine living without a car nowadays? It was very challenging, but you see, back where I grew up, it was very hard to even get a car; not only was it very expensive, but everyone who wanted one had to wait a very long time to get a car. I've known people that had to wait for years and years before they finally got their vehicle.

Nowadays, even in Germany, there are so many different kinds of cars to choose from. There are red VWs, silver Hondas, white Toyotas, black BMWs; the list goes on and on. But in East Germany, there were only a few types of vehicles to choose from: mainly Trabants and Wartburgs. Only those with very mysterious connections to even more mysterious people got to drive a Czech-manufactured Skoda. Only one person in our small village drove such a Skoda; it was bright-orange, and all the kids of the neighborhood thought it looked like a stylish racing car. But the other cars came in the dullest colors ever: a dirty white or a rusty brown. Occasionally, you'd see a light-blue or light-green Trabant, but that was very rare.

Because it took such a long time to get a car, everyone took great care of them if they had one. Every weekend, all the neighbors would be soaping down their cars, washing them until they were shiny and absolutely spotless.

But since we didn't have a vehicle, Omama and I walked everywhere. And I really mean everywhere. We walked to the grocery store. We walked to the bakery. My mom walked to her work and I walked to school. And once a month, Omama and I would walk all the way to the neighboring town called Schwarzenberg.

Schwarzenberg seemed like such an impressive metropolis compared to my little village. With its 16,000 residents, it had everything you could imagine: multiple grocery stores, restaurants, a library, a school, clothing stores, and even a department store. So, needless to say, a trip to Schwarzenberg was quite an adventure.

I learned early on that I always had to brace myself for a long walk. But Omama and I entertained ourselves by singing songs and telling each other stories which made the trips go faster. We carried all kinds of things on our way back home. Sometimes, we each carried full tote bags and backpacks. Other times, we lugged entire pieces of furniture all the way back to the village. Occasionally, when we knew we'd be buying something big, we would bring our blue trolley along and pull the load back home, with blisters on our hands when we got there.

I'm not quite sure why we didn't ride our bicycles to town. But since we had to take a big and busy road, I guess Omama thought it felt safer to just walk.

# 11
# MY LITTLE HIDEOUT

When I was little, I rode all over the yard on my tricycle. Then, when I was about 4 years old, Omama bought me a shiny blue bike with training wheels on it. I practiced riding it every day, until, one day, Omama decided to take the training wheels off. It took a couple of days and a couple of falls before I was able to balance my bike all on my own, but I eventually got it. Oh, was I proud! I couldn't ride fast enough. And when I got a little older, I got a bigger bike. I was so proud of it. It was also blue and very sparkly. I cleaned and polished it almost every weekend, while our neighbors polished their cars.

Omama and I stored our bikes in a small shed we had right next to our apartment house. Every apartment in our house had its own little shed. Ours was locked with a padlock on the door. I always had such a hard time unlocking it, because it was old and rusty. We also had a couple of tools and gardening items in this tiny wooden shack. I loved climbing behind the row of sheds; it made a great hideout whenever I played hide and seek with the neighborhood kids. Omama and I stored some wood and other bulky items behind the shed. During the summer, Omama would attach a tarp to the side of the shed and prop it up with stilts to create a covered, shady area.

Under it, she would pile our cut grass to dry so we would have hay for our bunnies in the winter months. I loved to jump and play in the hay.

## 12
## WE ALWAYS HAD PETS

Speaking of bunnies; did I tell you yet that we had all kinds of pets when I was little? We had parakeets and a guinea pig. We even had bunnies in the garden for a couple of years. And we always had cats. Sometimes, we'd have just one cat; and at other times, multiple cats at once. But they always stayed in grandma's apartment, not ours. When I was really little, before I could even talk or walk, we had this very black cat. He was actually very moody and sometimes mean and liked to hiss and show his sharp claws. But Omama told me that this cat was my biggest protector. He never scratched or hissed at me but always purred whenever he saw me.

Remember our apartment's toilet I told you about? With the big pipes that went straight into the sewer system? One winter, our cat fell into that toilet. Nobody noticed until we heard loud meowing and wailing. Luckily for our cat it was so cold that day that the inside of the toilet had a frozen layer of ice all around it. Our cat had dug its claws into the ice and held on for dear life. After we got him out of the toilet, he never stepped another paw into the bathroom again.

## 13
## MY KINDERGARTEN

When I was about 6 months old, Omama started taking me to a day nursery, called Kinderkrippe, and I stayed there all day while Omama was at work. It was pretty far away from where we lived, so it took Omama a long while to ride her bike there with me. She had a little wicker baby seat attached to her handlebar. She would bundle me up, buckle me into the seat, and ride along the bumpy, cobblestoned roads. 'Whwhwhwhwhwhwh,' I went, when we rode up and down the steep hills. Can you imagine doing this twice a day, every day, rain or shine?

I don't remember much about my Kinderkrippe days, only that they had huge wooden blocks that I would always play with. The other children and I would place them in a row, sit on them, and pretend to ride on a train. We had little train engineer and conductor costumes that we would take turns wearing. It was a fun game!

But I mostly remember my days I spent in kindergarten, which children in Germany start to go to when they are about three years old. Once they turn six, it's time for school. My kindergarten was a magical place. There were three separate rooms; one for all three-year-olds, one for four-year-olds, and one for five- and six-year-olds.

All day long, we'd play games, or work on art and craft projects, or make some loud music with small instruments, or listen to stories that the teachers would read to us. Everyone's favorite musical instrument was the shiny set of cymbals. It was the first gadget all kids rushed to when we were asked to pick an instrument. Unfortunately, we only had one set, so we had to wait patiently until it was our turn to play them. Then, we'd march in a circle in our room and make some earsplitting music.

We kids came to our kindergarten so early every morning that we would have to eat our breakfast there, which we brought with us from home. A typical German breakfast back then consisted of a cheese or cold-cut sandwich and some milk. Cereals did not exist in East Germany, not even cornflakes.

One day, I brought with me an interesting-looking sandwich. I remember Omama proudly packing it for me the night before, telling me that she bought some very special slices of ham. See, we didn't have much money back then, and things like ham were a pretty exceptional treat for Omama and I. This very special but also very chewy ham got me into a heap of trouble. One of our kindergarten rules was that we had to eat every single bite of the food we brought from home. I really tried to finish the entire sandwich, but the meat was just too chewy. No matter how much I champed and munched and chewed on that ham, it just didn't want to go down. And because it took me too long, our teacher put me in a separate room, telling me that I was not to come out until I ate the entire sandwich. I tried. I really did. But there was just no way! So instead of trying to eat it, I stashed the chunks of ham behind the heater of that room. I thought that this was a very clever hiding place. However, I did not take the ham's smell into consideration, because a couple of days later, the ham started to smell. Terribly! Following her nose, our teacher found the source of the foul smell. And because I had been the only one eating her breakfast in that room, everyone knew who put the ham there.

Omama never ever sent me with a ham sandwich to kindergarten again.

Lunch was delivered on a small, rusty truck every day. It had these huge covered pots on its back. The driver would carry the heavy containers inside and swap them with the empty containers that had held our lunch the day before. I must say that I wasn't a very big fan of our kindergarten lunches, but when I'm hungry, I'll eat almost anything, even then.

Once a week, a white van would come, open our big, red-painted metal gate, and back up into our kindergarten's driveway. The driver would then take out a bunch of very large linen sacks that held fresh towels and bedsheets. And before leaving, he would collect all our dirty towels and sheets and stuff them into the back of the van. We called him our laundry man. He was very friendly and always told us kids funny jokes that we tried to remember so we could retell them at home.

Going to the bathroom was a community effort, meaning we all went to the bathroom together. We would line up, receive a tiny piece of toilet paper from the teacher, and march into the large and open lavatory that had about eight little toilets; four on one wall, and another four on the opposite wall. All boys and girls had to sit down together and finish together. Afterwards, we'd wash our hands in one of the many tiny sinks lined up on another wall and march back into our room.

The trouble was, that the tiny piece of toilet paper we all got before going to the toilet really was so unbelievably small. It was never enough for the more serious bathroom events. Let's just say that I hope that you will always have enough paper on hand.

Our kindergarten had a really fun and bright playground. We had a metal slide, a metal seesaw, some serious monkey bars, and an incredibly huge sandbox – much bigger than mine at home. The sandbox in our kindergarten was so gigantic and so deep that we could have used it as a swimming pool if we would have filled it with water instead of sand. No matter how deep we would dig, not one of us ever reached the very bottom. Needless to say, we had lots of fun in that sandbox. There were also a whole bunch of swings on which we tried to outswing and outjump each other.

Behind the swings was an old wooden fence. And behind the fence was an entire row of various bushes with the most delicious-looking berries. The trouble was that these bushes with the delicious-looking berries belonged to the person that lived right next to our kindergarten. We saw the berries every time we went outside. So one time I couldn't resist any longer. I had to try these berries and see if they really were as delicious as they looked. I skillfully snuck my way to the fence, looked around to make sure no one would see me, and reached through the fence. I plucked a whole handful of berries from one of the bushes and stuffed them into my mouth as fast as I could. Mmmh, were they yummy! Just as delicious as I had thought they would be!

As I rolled my eyes with delight, I heard someone say, "Delicious, aren't they?"

Surprised, I turned around and saw the owner of the

berry bushes standing right next to them on the other side of the fence. She'd been there all along, watching me gulp down her juicy berries. I was so embarrassed that I quickly turned around and ran away. I never tried any of the delicious berries again. Not a single one.

# 14
# AN OLD GERMAN TRADITION

Right after I turned seven (my birthday is in June), I started first grade. I know that starting kindergarten is a tremendous event in America, but in Germany it is the first grade that marks the beginning of all school years to come; so it is celebrated with all sorts of great traditions.

One of these traditions is the school cone. Filled to the brim with candy and small gifts, this colorfully decorated cone made my heart beat so fast with excitement. My school cone had colorful illustrations of American Indians on it. It showed their horses, teepees and roaring campfires. It had a beautiful bow on top and was very heavy, full of special gifts just for me. I couldn't wait to see what was in it! As soon as I came home from my very first day of first grade, I threw my new (and heavy!) leather satchel full of all my new books into the corner of the room, tore off the bow on top of my school cone and dumped the entire contents onto our couch. All I remember happening after that is wild unwrapping and delightful munching and chewing of all the candy I found inside. It was a glorious day!

## 15
## MY DAILY COMMUTE

Omama had to be at work very early every morning, even before any rooster bothered to crow. And because she had to start her day so early, I had to tag along and spend a couple of hours with her at work before school. Omama worked in our local, very old railway station selling train tickets. Back then, lots of people used the train to get to work, so her job was very important.

The sun was still asleep when we slipped into the train station through the heavy back door. I was always very excited, especially when I got to use the old but fancy-looking ticket printing machine. Each train stop had its own cylindrical printer drum, so depending on where a passenger wanted to go, Omama would pick the corresponding printer drum, insert it into the ticket printing machine and turn it. The machine would then make a loud stamping sound, shake a little, and spit the cardboard-thick ticket out the bottom. I felt very important whenever I was allowed to find the correct drum and print tickets for passengers.

Whenever a train was approaching, Omama had to rush outside and block off the passage way to make sure none of the passengers could run across the tracks.

Remember when I told you that we didn't have a car? Well, we didn't have school buses back then, either. That meant that I had to walk to school every single day, rain or shine; blizzard or hail, and most of it uphill. It took me about 40 minutes to walk all by myself from Omama's place of work all the way to my school. I walked passed my old kindergarten, passed my teacher's house and passed the mayor's window in the city hall. When I saw the tall bell tower, I knew I'd almost made it to school.

# 16
# I LOVED SCHOOL

I loved school. I loved every single class. Math class, music class, writing class, gym class, art class – I found everything so interesting. We even had a gardening class. Our school had a beautiful garden right next to the main building. The garden was full of flowerbeds and fruit trees, and there was a greenhouse and a big shed, which held all the gardening tools. During gardening class, we had to pull weeds, cut the bushes, or harvest the apples and plums from the trees. I learned so much about flowers, vegetables, and fruit.

During one fall, we all had to grab a bucket and walk to the nearby forest. It was quite a hike. But once we got far enough into the woods, our teacher showed us an enormous ditch in the ground; it was almost as big as a crater. And the best part was that it was completely filled with dead leaves that had fallen from the surrounding trees. The entire time we were there, everyone would take it in turns making a running start and jumping into the pool of leaves. We had so much fun that we almost forgot to return to school. Before we set back off, we all filled our buckets with dead leaves and carried them back to our school garden, where we dumped them onto our compost. By the next spring, all those leaves had turned into nourishing dirt that enriched all our flowerbeds.

## 17
## BE READY – ALWAYS READY

I was a very proud Young Pioneer in Germany, which is very similar to Boy and Girl Scouts. I had my very own uniform, consisting of a white shirt and a blue triangular necktie. It took me a lot of practice to learn how to tie the knot of the necktie just right. We wore our uniform to school festivals and Young Pioneer events. Each year, we would get new pins for good grades, excellent behavior and for being a great example for others. I was highly decorated with all kinds of medals and pins.

Each pioneer had to have an ID pass with a photo. This little booklet had important pioneer commandments, which we needed to memorize by heart. We even had our very own slogan, "Be ready – always ready," which we would recite every morning before the beginning of class.

As a pioneer, we participated in all kinds of contests. We had recycling competitions in which we tried to collect as much paper and glass as possible. Every time we would bring recyclables to the recycling center, they would weigh them and put the weight into our booklet. Whoever had the most weight at the end of the school year would earn a reward. We also participated in many sport and science competitions. We were proud to represent our school wherever we went.

As a Young Pioneer I learned about Yuri Gagarin, a Russian Soviet pilot and cosmonaut. He was the first human to journey into outer space. We followed the news about Nelson Mandela, a South African revolutionary who was sent to prison for believing in equality. And we anxiously awaited and cheered for the annual Peace Race, a multistage bicycle race. Every morning, we would report which bicyclist was currently leading and would note it on a race leader board we'd created especially for this event. Our teachers taught us to be proud of our country and to honor it by being dutiful and obedient young pioneers.

# 18
# LUNCH STUBS

At school, every grade had lunch together at the same time, which always created a huge queue and backlog. All students of all classes would race up the hill to our cafeteria as fast as they could, trying to beat everyone to it. Our cafeteria was quite large, with many tables and chairs. It was located on the second floor, right next to the extended care area. Every day, we had to wait in this huge line, which wound itself all the way from the outside of the building, through the door, up the stairs, into the cafeteria and all the way to the window where they would hand out the food. So if it rained and I got a late start walking up to the cafeteria, I usually ended up being completely soaked from waiting in line outside of the building.

Before entering the cafeteria on top of the stairs, one of the teachers would stand next to the door, check our hands to make sure they were clean, and collect our meal ticket stubs, which we had to purchase at the beginning of every week. Then we would march to the window, where the kitchen's cook would stand and hand out our meal. It was usually one main meal, a small dessert like canned fruit, and water. No seconds. We would take our trays and find a place to sit. Usually, I tried to find a place to sit with my classmates, so we could all chat together.

After the meal was eaten, we had to clean up by walking to the back of the cafeteria. One of the teachers would stand there to make sure that we had eaten enough of our food. If there were still too many leftovers on my plate, the teacher would send me back to eat more. Once I made it through this check point, I had to scrape the remainder of my food into a big container. This container was called the piggy bin. Every house, actually, had such a piggy bin. All food scraps and leftovers were picked up every other day and used to feed pigs and other farm animals. Food didn't go to waste.

## 19
## IMPOSSIBLE TO CHOOSE

Though I loved all my classes, I especially loved art class! Every now and then when the weather was nice, our teacher would have us grab our drawing pads and some pencils and would hold our class outside so we could draw the wonderful things we saw around us. I also loved my music class. Sometimes we would listen to music, and other times, we'd sing throughout the entire class. But I also enjoyed my gym class, where we would run around the field, playing soccer or dodgeball.

During recess, we'd go outside and play catch or 'Simon Says,' or we would just sit on the wall next to the schoolhouse and eat our sandwiches and drink our milk. Drinking our milk was always tricky; we didn't have cartons like you do. Our milk came in a little plastic bag. Once you poked the straw through the bag, you couldn't set it down anywhere without the milk leaking out of it. So once it was opened, you had to finish the entire bag. The younger kids always tried to copy the older kids in the upper classes. Those kids wouldn't use their straws at all, but simply chew a hole in one of the corners of their bags and drink their milk that way. We little kids thought it was the coolest thing.

I liked all my classes. But did you know that in East Germany I also had to go to school on Saturdays? We only had a couple of classes that day, but I had to walk all the way to school and back home just the same. I guess our teachers were trying to keep us out of trouble, even on the weekends.

After school, I always had to go to extended care, since Omama had to work until late every afternoon. First, we'd have tea and a snack together, and then everyone would sit down and do their homework. I enjoyed going to extended care, because I got my homework done even before going home. And afterwards, we kids would play together. I remember one time when we prepared a play for our caretakers. We created a stage and put chairs around it, and then performed a really fun show, pretending to be circus acrobats.

Sometimes in extended care we worked on craft projects; or we just played with the many toys. And once it was time to go home, one of the caretakers would send me on my way.

## 20
## OUR FORT IN THE WOODS

My friends always considered me to be one of the best fort builders they'd ever known. It was true, I suppose. Give me a bunch of branches, sticks and leaves, and I could have built anything. The best fort my friends and I ever built was in a little forest island on top of a hill, right next to an old farm. It was a cute farm right on the edge of our tiny village. They had a small dog that we were allowed to play with. So sometimes, we'd pick him up and take him with us into the woods. We'd pretend to be some sort of settlers that had to grow their own food and build their own home. Our little forest island was perfect.

We called it an island, because it looked like a forest-covered patch of land in the middle of a green hill. Between a number of trees was a rocky mound. We used the top of the mound as our lookout, and on the bottom of it we built our fort, using large branches and sticks.

We went and worked on it a little bit every day. Right after school, we would pick up the dog and run up the grassy hill to our slowly growing fort in the forest island. We'd bring pots and pans, blankets and other things from our homes that we needed to build our settlement. We had so much fun.

To protect our fort, we built a bunch of traps all along the edge of the forest. We dug deep holes, filled them with the dog's droppings or fresh cow pies and covered them back up with sticks and branches. And it worked! We knew, because sometimes we'd find our traps with the sticks on the top broken and visible footprints on the stinky manure. Our traps kept any intruder away.

# 21
## OH CHRISTMAS TREE

Christmas was one of my favorite holidays when I was little. And it still is. My anticipation for Christmas started on the first day of December with the opening of the very first door of my Christmas calendar. A Christmas calendar has exactly 24 doors; one for each of the days until Christmas. A traditional calendar has a little piece of chocolate hidden behind each of these doors.

On the night before December 6th, I would pick one of my biggest winter boots, polish and shine it, and place it outside my front door. Legend has it, that St Nicholas comes that night to fill the boots with coal for naughty kids, and candy and other small goodies for all well-behaved children, so you would know what sort of presents to expect on Christmas Day. The next morning, I would excitedly run to my boot at the front door and find it stuffed to the brim with chocolates and nuts.

Did you know that the tradition of setting up and decorating a Christmas tree comes from Germany? But not as early as we do in America. In our home in Germany, the Christmas tree was put up the night before Christmas Day. Christmas Eve was also the time to open our presents. It was always such a wondrous, happy time. Each of us would have a little plate sitting underneath the Christmas tree, filled with chocolate Santa Clauses, almonds, walnuts, hazelnuts, chocolate coins, and oranges. I loved how we would sit around our opened presents, cracking and eating nuts together. The dim lights wrapped around our Christmas tree always created such a warm atmosphere on that very special night.

## 22
## SEEING THE WORLD – OR NOT

Since Omama did not have a car, we did not get to travel very much. But we did visit family quite regularly using the train. We didn't have internet back then to look up train timetables, so we had to use something called a Course Book, which would list all the arrival and departure times of all train stations of the entire country. So if there was no direct train going from our station to the station we wanted to travel to, we would first have to figure out what connecting trains to take to get us there. Omama was really good at finding the best and fastest travel plans for us. She did work at the train station, after all.

We then would purchase our tickets and hop on the train. I would bring along books to read on our journey, a couple of drawing pens and some paper to keep myself entertained during the long hours on the train. But usually I got so sleepy from the musical clickety-clacking of the train against the tracks that I fell asleep within the first half-hour. I only woke up whenever the conductor came along to punch a hole into new passengers' tickets with his hole puncher.

Travel in our German Democratic Republic was quite restricted by political circumstances of the day. East Germans mostly traveled throughout their own countryside. The most popular vacation spots back when I was little were the beaches along the Baltic Sea. Omama and I never made it there, but my friends would send me colorful postcards and return with an abundance of seashells and other wonderful souvenirs to let me know that I had not been forgotten during their summer vacations.

## 23
## EVERYTHING CHANGES

In the very beginning of my stories I told you that the country I grew up in does not exist any longer. When I was 10 years old, East Germany and West Germany became one country, which today is known simply as Germany. With the union of those two countries, my life and everything I had known until then changed. People began driving different cars. Stores had new vegetables and fruits I had never seen before. All of a sudden, we were able to buy as many bananas as we wanted to. Stores had more variety, so we could choose from ten different jams, or ten different breads, or ten different soups. The varieties seemed endless.

I remember feeling so overwhelmed by all the new things around me. For the first time in my life, I learned about Mickey Mouse, and Coca Cola, and McDonald's. I was introduced to magazines with colorful and shiny paper. I couldn't believe how beautiful these pages looked and felt.

Our rough and dull toilet paper was replaced by soft, tissue-like paper. I never knew toilet paper could be so smooth. Phone cable was placed throughout our little village so that people could have their own phones. People began purchasing new TV sets to watch gameshows and TV series that I didn't even know existed. The radio played songs in English, a language I'd never heard before. And even though I didn't know what the singers were singing, I thought the music sounded beautiful.

In school, we learned about America and England. We talked about the Beetles and other stars we didn't know about before. We began using a different kind of money. The new coins felt heavy and looked so polished.

People began traveling out of East Germany, and all over the world, trying to see what they had only heard about before. And while some returned, many did not. They were too mesmerized by the new possibilities and opportunities this reunification brought with it. For better or for worse, our lives were forever changed.

Those were the days of my childhood. I remember them fondly. I may not have had much, but I had a loving family, a nice and cozy home, and many caring people around me. And I couldn't ask for anything more than that.

And now it's your turn! I can't wait to hear all your exciting and wonderful stories.

## ABOUT THE AUTHOR

Yvonne Jones was born in former East Germany to a German mother and a Vietnamese father. Thus, she spent an inordinate amount of her youth nosing through books that she shouldn't have been reading, and watching movies that she shouldn't have been watching. It was a good childhood.

She currently lives in Texas with her husband and their two sons. In theory, she is working on her next children's book. In reality, she is probably being tickled or busy pretend-playing with her little ones. She can be found online at **www.Yvonne-Jones.com**.

YVONNE JONES

**Photo credits**
Cover, Sveta Gaintseva/Shutterstock; 1, Yvonne Jones; 4, Nichole Schmidt/Shutterstock; 6, Bundesarchiv, Bild 183-1985-1012-087/CC-BY-SA; 8, Kirsten Wagner/Shutterstock; 11, Bundesarchiv, Bild 183-1984-1126-312/CC-BY-SA; 15, Bundearchiv, Bild 183-PO619-306/Ludwig, Juergen/CC-BY-SA; 19, Yvonne Jones; 20, Bundesarchiv, Bild 183-1989-0710-025/LPG Merxleben/CC-BY-SA; 23, Bundesarchiv, Bild 183-F0818-0013-001/CC-BY-SA; 24, Yvonne Jones; 26, Ludwig Klein/Getty Images; 28, Yvonne Jones; 29, Andrea Ulbrich/Shutterstock; 30, Bundesarchiv, Bild 183-1987-0523-032/Jan Peter Kasper/CC-BY-SA; 30, NASA/CC; 30, U.S. Congress/CC; 36, Bundesarchiv, Bild 183-1987-0109-028/Grubitzsch, Waltraud/CC-BY-SA; 38, Bundesarchiv, Bild 183-1989-1112-009/Paetzold, Ralf/CC-BY-SA

Made in United States
North Haven, CT
15 May 2023

36604155R00032